AF496470

GP1

Matador
9 Priory Business Park,
Wistow Road, Kibworth Beauchamp,
Leicestershire. LE8 0RX
Tel: 0116 279 2299
Email: books@troubador.co.uk
Web: www.troubador.co.uk/matador
Twitter: @matadorbooks

ISBN 978 1788039 697

British Library Cataloguing in Publication Data.
A catalogue record for this book is available from the British Library.

Printed and bound by CPI Group (UK) Ltd, Croydon, CR0 4YY
Typeset in 11pt Cambria by Troubador Publishing Ltd, Leicester, UK

Matador is an imprint of Troubador Publishing Ltd

To my own guinea pigs Toby and Robin

Happy reading
Andy

Monday

6:25 a.m.

I was woken up by heavy footsteps and the kitchen door flew open with a tremendous crash. The bright light clicked on. The shadowy man spoke: "Oh!" he exclaimed, speaking to no one in particular. "Who hasn't done the washing up?" He looked accusingly at the kitchen sink, full to the brim with last night's dirty dinner things. One of the plates seemed to wobble a little, almost in fright, and settle further into the brown, murky water, as if to hide from the verbal onslaught.

6:26 a.m.

Having stared at the sink for a few moments, the man then looked in my direction, his eyes menacing. I hid nervously in the safety of my tube. He didn't seem to be in a very good mood. "Where are you?" he said, his eyes probing the straw in my cage. The tense silence was broken when the clock ticked loudly.

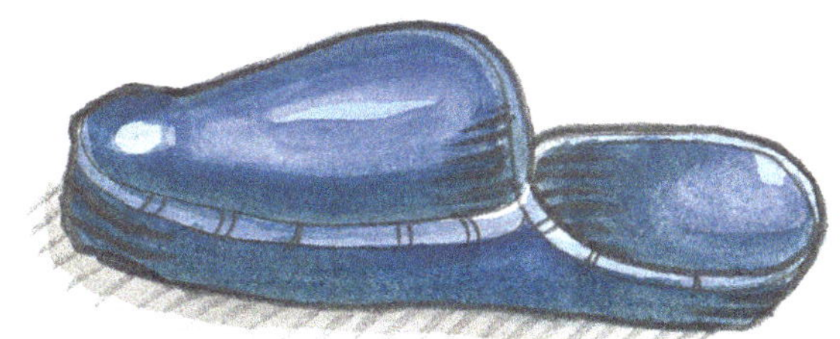

6:27 a.m.

Then he started to make the usual 'clucking' noises. I didn't answer, staying safely under cover. He came even closer, accidently catching the toe of his slipper on the edge of my cage, making me jump. He spoke again: "Ah! You **have** been a good boy, haven't you? You've done all your poos in the corner." Oh! How embarrassing.

6:28 a.m.

I heard the kettle switch on.

6:30 a.m.

I heard the kettle switch off. Fluffy white steam rose in wispy bunches to cling, blanket like, to the kitchen ceiling. The steam seemed to creep along the ceiling towards a window that was slightly open, then escape.

Perhaps the steam would join together with other steam and then, when it was big enough, join together and make a cloud. Is that how clouds are made? Anyway, it reminded me of my dream last night...

I dreamt I was a Pilot...

A famous flyer who's in a fix,
When danger arose I'd lick my lips.
A dangerous flight in stormy weather,
My plane tossed around like the lightest feather.

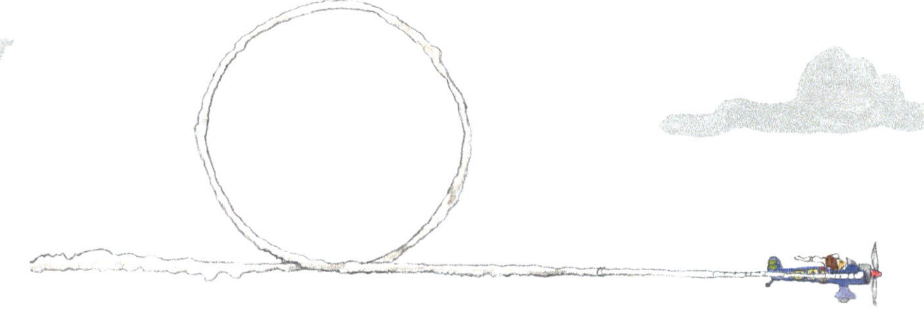

Loop the loop as the thunder crashed,
The rudder hard over as the rain drops lashed.
A pull on the stick as the last muscle strained,
Doing the things for which I was trained.

Peering into the darkness, it was blacker than black.
"Here we go now, there's no turning back!"
And finally taming the storm and the rage,
I made it at last, although it seemed like an age.

Eventually gliding in silence to land,
On a beach in the sunset, soft in the sand,
And coolly I'd stroll, barefoot in the wavelets,
Just one more story in the history of brave pets.

Tuesday

Overcast, rain in most regions. Put more hay in guinea pig cages.

6:23 a.m.

I was woken up by the toilet flushing - someone's up early!

6:24 a.m.

The kitchen door opened with a **whoosh** of air and the light went on with a sharp **click**. The man looked directly at me. I was caught in the open. I stared at him. He stared at me. I stared back at him. He stared back at me. I had seen this sort of thing on the television in the kitchen. 'Cowboys', I think they were called. They did a lot of staring at each other.

I tried to beat my record for 'standing still and staring'. I checked the clock on the wall. 12.8 seconds; not quite my best but a good effort all the same.

I wondered if there was a *Guinea Pig Book of World Records*. Perhaps I could become famous.

4:10 p.m.

I'm in disgrace. I was sitting on Toby's lap - he's the big boy of the family - when I accidentally nibbled his finger. I was sure it was a carrot. Same shape, same size, almost the same colour. You can understand the confusion. Of course, there was a lot of panic.

4:11 p.m.

Anyway, I've been grounded for a week. No more cuddles. No more strokes, no more 'clucking' sounds. To pass the time I've been working out how many days there are in a week. And then how many hours there are in a day. And then how many minutes there are in an hour.

I was working out how many seconds there are in a minute when all these numbers reminded me of my dream last night…

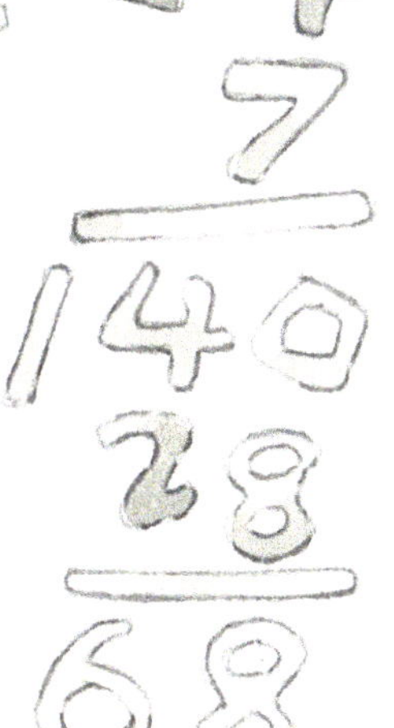

I dreamt I was a Mathematician...

The greatest mathematician in the class,
In addition and subtraction, I was fast.
My numbers divided and multiplied,
As if by magic before my eyes.

Tricky sums on lined paper grew,
Tricky shapes on graph paper I drew.
Sometimes using an accurate stencil,
Often having to sharpen my pencil.

From friends and family, I received their thanks,
For advising on their guinea piggy banks.
As my reputation climbed even higher,
I decided to purchase the correct attire

With a bowler hat and leather briefcase,
Financial problems I would gladly face,
With pinstriped trousers and shiny black shoes,
In the Guinea Pig Times, I was front page news.

9

Wednesday

6:42 a.m.

I was woken up by the milkman. Nice man, but I'm sure he doesn't need to make that much noise with just two milk bottles. I wondered what the milk tastes like.

7:20 a.m.

Today I learnt how to vibrate. It's not something I'd practised, it just sort of happens! I hunch myself up and start to shake, making a sort of buzzing noise! I decided to try it again sometime.

7:31 a.m.

The opportunity came a little more quickly than I had planned. All the family were sitting at the breakfast table when I saw my chance. I concentrated, started shaking and made the buzzing noise right there and then. It made quite a scene.

"What's that?" someone said.

"It's the water pipes!" said someone else.

"No, it's the fridge, I told you we needed a new one!" said the lady.

"Surely it's the dishwasher?" said the man. "Let's listen carefully and see if it happens again."

There was absolute silence in the room while they all listened. I was absolutely silent in my cage while I watched them. I'm going to keep my clever trick a secret and save it for special occasions.

7:35 a.m.

I retreated into my tube, with my breakfast lettuce leaf, feeling rather pleased with myself. On the way, I accidently trod on the edge of my food bowl and spilt the 'Good Boy' cereal (for healthy teeth) all over the floor of my cage. The spillage made a rather interesting, artistic pattern, which reminded me of my dream last night…

I dreamt I was an Artist...

A famous artist to rival Picasso,
A trendy smock and a beret worn so low,
Careful brushwork on canvas or paper,
My creative ideas in thick paint forever.

Bright red crimson and cobalt blue,
With yellow ochre of pleasing hue,
Greens and purples and white of twelve shades,
Just the right mix on the palette was made.

The papers were full of critical acclaim,
From humble beginnings to wondrous fame.
A famous face from Paris to London,
Well on the way to my new-found stardom.

Paintings displayed in the national galleries,
A foundation set up for guinea pig charities.
A star-studded career in the future was set,
Not a bad effort for a small, furry pet.

Thursday

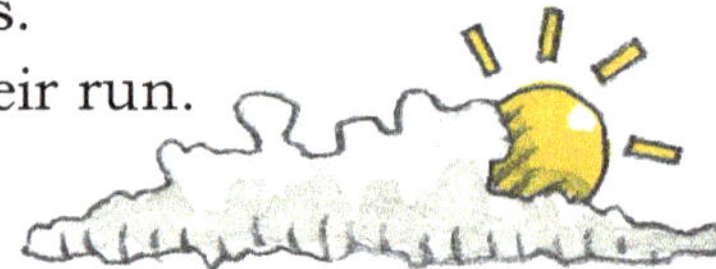

6:51 a.m.

I was woken up by some noisy birds at the window: common hedge sparrows. I recognised them from the poster on the wall in the kitchen. The picture of the sparrow is next to the one of the robin, the one that Toby has drawn the glasses on! Toby's little brother is called Robin!

6:52 a.m.

My lettuce leaf arrived early this morning. I dragged it into my tube. "You **are** a hungry boy, aren't you?" said the man. The man thought for a moment and then continued: "Honey!" he said to his wife. "Is the guinea pig a boy or a girl?"

Oh really! Isn't it obvious? I fluffed myself up to look really big and manly, just to make the point.

6:55 a.m.

I've been practising making patterns
with my teeth on the lettuce leaves.
I've almost perfected how to make
little heart shaped cut outs and
yesterday I chewed out the shape
of a skateboard, just like the one
the man tripped over in the kitchen
the other day! One day I'll complete a picture this way.

I'll call it **Daffodils in Bloom.** That's the name
on the postcard on the pin board on the wall above my
cage. I prefer it to the one that fell into my cage, the one
that I chewed to bits. That was called **Sunset Over
Hastings Pier.**

7:01 a.m.

Anyway, it's time to get back
to my lettuce leaf patterns
and this reminded me of my
dream last night…

I dreamt I was a Gardener...

Butterflies loved my summery glades,
Dragonflies hovered on the breezes they'd made,
Bumble bees bumbled into flowery flower heads,
Glow worms lit up the dark skies before bed.

Six types of lettuce, or seven or nine,
Herbs like tarragon, rosemary and thyme,
Cabbage occasionally, with parsley my favourite,
I'd always take time to sit down and savour it.

Gardeners praised my greenhouse and borders,
Seed trays and plant pots arranged in neat order,
Cucumber, carrots and spinach all growing,
But the grass, rather cleverly, didn't need mowing.

My dream about cutting the grass is worth knowing,
There's no huffing or puffing or hard work or yelling,
The thin bit, the thick bit, the long and the short of it
Was taken care of by friends, who happily ate all of it!

Friday

6:58 a.m.

I was woken up by a storm outside. The wind brought lashing rain through the terrified trees. The leaves were racing around in a manic dance on the ground. It wasn't the time to be active. Anyway, there might be something good on the television in the kitchen.

5:10 p.m.

I've been busy this afternoon flicking things with my nose. After some practice, I managed to flick my food bowl right the way over! I can also nudge my tube over to different sides of my cage.

I played a little game. I moved my tube to one side of the cage, waited until someone noticed and when they stopped looking I moved it back again. It was good fun!

5:45 p.m.

I've just heard something really interesting. Katie (that's Robin's friend) is coming to our house tomorrow for an 'over sleep'. I think I heard it correctly! And she is bringing her pet with her. How cool is that? The trouble is that I don't know what sort of pet she has. However, I have decided to be on my best behaviour and display my best manners. This means no noisy water-dripper slurping, no snatching food and I must tidy my cage. Well, maybe not the last one!

6:00 p.m.

The lady was clearing up the kitchen and all was going well when suddenly: "Oh, blast! And double blast! And bother! And double bother!" she exclaimed. I have cleaned up the language a little for my younger readers! She was very angry. She had spilt a large bowl of soapy water on the floor.

The water had surged over the floor like a small tidal wave and risen up at the edge of my cage, only to recede in ever decreasing wavelets. This reminded me of my dream last night...

I dreamt I was a Surfer...

I'd travel each year to Cornwall or Devon,
In a cool camper van with my board, it was heaven.
I'd park on the beach, near the kiosk and ice cream,
I'd wink to the lifeguards and the rest of the brave team.

I'd meet up with friends, and raise up a cup,
Then we'd shout loudly together the famous "Surf's up!"
We'd gaze out to sea and laugh at the breeze,
My Bermuda shorts were a bit of a squeeze!

The water was clear, a dab tickled my cold toes,
The salty spray swirled and tickled my cold nose.
We'd wade through the small waves and wait for a big one,
There's nothing quite like it, all sand, sea and bright sun.

And then we'd sit in a group, using surfboards as windbreaks,
We'd barbeque courgettes on a wood fire from old crates,
We'd pull on a jumper and sip carrot juice with cream,
We'd plan to meet next year and meanwhile, surf in our dreams.

Saturday

4:42 a.m.

I couldn't wait to wake up. I was so excited. I looked out of my cage but it was completely dark, except for the moon, which shone through the window in a comforting glow. I thought of possible ways to wake everybody up but, in the end, I just waited. And waited. And waited. And after that… I just waited.

3:30 p.m.

The day had dragged on and on and then suddenly I heard the doorbell ring. This was the moment I had been waiting for. The arrival of Robin's friend and her pet for their 'over sleep'. But what sort of pet would it be?

Could it be a cat? That would be no good. Could it be a dog? Not much better, might be a bit too big and maybe a bit smelly! Could it be a rabbit? I quite like rabbits. Yes, probably a rabbit. I hoped it wasn't a tarantula!

3:35 p.m.

The two young children burst noisily into the kitchen, laughing and giggling. They peered into my cage. I put on my cutest look. "That's my one!" said Robin, pointing at me. "I'll go and get mine!" said his friend Katie, who ran off to get her pet. I checked the clock. She reappeared in 9.2 seconds. Umm! Not bad. I made a mental note for my **Guinea Pig Book of World Records.**

3:36 p.m.

Katie lifted the lid off the small cage. I held my breath. There was a small squeal as the animal was lifted out. I recognised the sound. The unmistakable sound of another… **guinea pig!** Toenails scrabbled as my very own 'over sleep' friend touched down for a safe landing in my cage, amongst a flurry of sawdust. I was very excited. I raced this way and that and jumped over my bowl.

I moon-walked backwards into each corner of my cage and then back to the centre and did a 360. My new friend looked at me and then nuzzled in the hay, found my last lettuce reserves and ate them! I didn't mind and, anyway, all this activity reminded me of my dream last night…

I dreamt I was a Dancer...

Many mice had learnt to prance,
Even a gerbil had learnt a stance,
But given the opportunity and chance,
This fine guinea pig had learnt to dance.

Long hours of practice in front of a mirror,
A shimmer, a shake, a twirl and a shiver,
Finally, the day came for hard competition,
All of my hard work came to splendid fruition.

The hired band made an infernal racket,
But with lucky seven upon my jacket,
I waltzed and fox trotted and did the samba,
With only one thing the slightest hamper…

…all on my own I danced those dances,
Far too shy to take those chances,
I promised myself next time I'll ask her.
Yes, in my next dream, I'll find a partner.

Sunday

Bright sunshine, rising temperatures, guinea pigs may need to cool off.

8:30 a.m.

We were woken up by the telephone ringing. The man opened the kitchen door and grabbed the telephone roughly from its home on the wall. "Yes? Yes?" he answered. It was Katie's mum on the line. "Yes, oh, yes, they're fine, they survived the night," he continued. And then, looking our way, he reassured the caller: "Yes, yes, the guinea pigs are fine too." He gave a second look in our direction. We both gave him a kind of 'oh really' expression, as if to say they need not have worried.

10:00 a.m.

Katie's mum arrived and collected her daughter together with my 'over sleep' friend. Wow! We had a great time. We stayed up late, swapping stories and sharing a midnight feast of cucumber chunks and carrot sticks. We listened to an owl in the tree next door. He was calling to a friend and the friend was answering back. We watched as the moon rose above the tree line and shone pale grey half-light through the window. We listened to the breeze as it gently teased the branches and then sent us to sleep. I wonder what I'll dream about tonight?

Sweet dreams.

27